Success With

Fractions

SCHOLASTIC

Editor: Ourania Papacharalambous
Cover design by Tannaz Fassihi; cover illustration by Kevin Zimmer
Interior design by Mina Chen
Interior illustrations by Carol Michael Denman (7–8, 11–12, 14, 22, 29, 34, 37, 41, 45–46);
Doug Jones (6, 18, 21, 26); Mike Moran (32)
All other images © Shutterstock.com

ISBN 978-1-338-79836-4
Scholastic Inc., 557 Broadway, New York, NY 10012
Copyright © 2022 Scholastic Inc.
All rights reserved. Printed in the U.S.A.
First printing, January 2022
2 3 4 5 6 7 8 9 10   40   29 28 27 26 25 24 23

INTRODUCTION

Parents and teachers alike will find *Scholastic Success With Fractions* to be a valuable resource. Students will enjoy completing a wide variety of engaging activities as they sharpen their skills with fractions. On page 4, you will find a list of the key skills covered in the activities throughout this book. Remember to praise students for their efforts and successes!

TABLE OF CONTENTS

Grade-Appropriate Skills Covered in *Scholastic Success With Fractions: Grade 4*

Explain why a fraction a/b is equivalent to a fraction $(n \times a)/(n \times b)$ by using visual fraction models, with attention to how the number and size of the parts differ even though the two fractions themselves are the same size. Use this principle to recognize and generate equivalent fractions.

Compare two fractions with different numerators and different denominators, e.g., by creating common denominators or numerators, or by comparing to a benchmark fraction such as 1/2. Recognize that comparisons are valid only when the two fractions refer to the same whole. Record the results of comparisons with symbols >, =, or <, and justify the conclusions, e.g., by using a visual fraction model.

Understand addition and subtraction of fractions as joining and separating parts referring to the same whole.

Decompose a fraction into a sum of fractions with the same denominator in more than one way, recording each decomposition by an equation. Justify decompositions, e.g., by using a visual fraction model.

Add and subtract mixed numbers with like denominators, e.g., by replacing each mixed number with an equivalent fraction, and/or by using properties of operations and the relationship between addition and subtraction.

Solve word problems involving addition and subtraction of fractions referring to the same whole and having like denominators, e.g., by using visual fraction models and equations to represent the problem.

Understand a fraction a/b as a multiple of $1/b$. For example, use a visual fraction model to represent 5/4 as the product $5 \times (1/4)$, recording the conclusion by the equation $5/4 = 5 \times (1/4)$.

Understand a multiple of a/b as a multiple of $1/b$, and use this understanding to multiply a fraction by a whole number. For example, use a visual fraction model to express $3 \times (2/5)$ as $6 \times (1/5)$, recognizing this product as 6/5. (In general, $n \times (a/b) = (n \times a)/b$.)

What Is a Fraction?

A fraction consists of two parts.

 $\frac{3}{4}$ The **numerator** tells how many parts are being identified.
The **denominator** tells the total number of equal parts in the whole.

Write what fraction of each figure is shaded.

1

_____   _____   _____   _____

2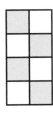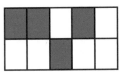

_____   _____   _____   _____

3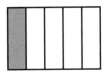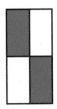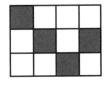

_____   _____   _____   _____

4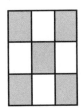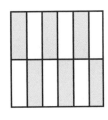

_____   _____   _____

Shade Is Cool!

Shade each figure to show the fraction.

1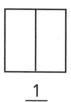

$\frac{1}{2}$ $\frac{2}{6}$

2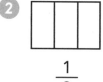

$\frac{1}{3}$ $\frac{5}{6}$ $\frac{3}{5}$

3

$\frac{5}{9}$ $\frac{4}{8}$ $\frac{1}{4}$ $\frac{7}{8}$ $\frac{3}{4}$

4

$\frac{7}{10}$ $\frac{3}{7}$ $\frac{7}{16}$ $\frac{4}{5}$ $\frac{9}{14}$

 Megan has a blue-and-white beach umbrella. On another sheet of paper, draw a picture of the umbrella to show 6 blue parts and 6 white parts. Be sure each part is the same size.

A Racing Set

A group of something can be considered one whole set. For example, let's pretend we have a group of 7 people. Five are boys, and the rest are girls.

What fraction are boys? $\dfrac{5}{7}$ What fraction are girls? $\dfrac{2}{7}$

Write a fraction for the shaded part of each set.

1. _____

2. _____

3. _____

4. _____

5. _____

6. _____

Scholastic Success With Fractions • Grade 4   **7**

Shaded Fractions

Shade in the fraction for each set.

1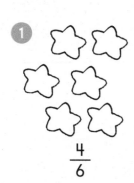
$\frac{4}{6}$

2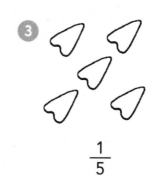
$\frac{4}{9}$

3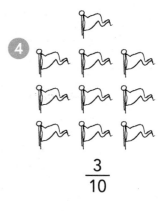
$\frac{1}{5}$

4
$\frac{3}{10}$

5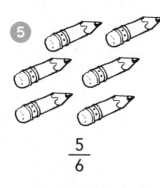
$\frac{5}{6}$

6
$\frac{7}{12}$

7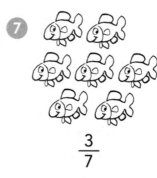
$\frac{3}{7}$

8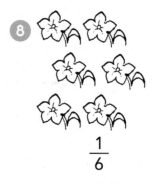
$\frac{1}{6}$

9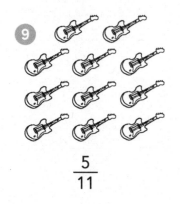
$\frac{5}{11}$

10
$\frac{1}{3}$

11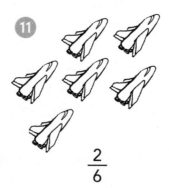
$\frac{2}{6}$

12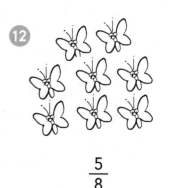
$\frac{5}{8}$

Draw a set and shade in part to show each fraction.

13 $\frac{3}{4}$

14 $\frac{7}{8}$

15 $\frac{4}{5}$

It's All the Same!

Equivalent fractions have the same amount.

 $\frac{1}{2} = \frac{4}{8}$ $\frac{3}{6} = \frac{1}{2}$

Write each missing numerator to show equivalent fractions.

1

$\frac{1}{2} = \frac{}{4}$

2

$\frac{1}{3} = \frac{}{6}$

3
$\frac{1}{4} = \frac{}{8}$

4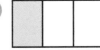
$\frac{1}{3} = \frac{}{9}$

5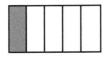
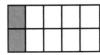
$\frac{1}{5} = \frac{}{10}$

6
$\frac{1}{2} = \frac{}{8}$

7

$\frac{1}{2} = \frac{}{16}$

8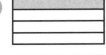

$\frac{1}{4} = \frac{}{20}$

Write the number sentence that shows each set of equivalent fractions.

9
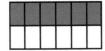
$\frac{}{} = \frac{}{}$

10
$\frac{}{} = \frac{}{}$

11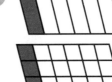
$\frac{}{} = \frac{}{}$

12
$\frac{}{} = \frac{}{}$

Where Do We Draw the Line?

A number line can be used to identify equivalent fractions.

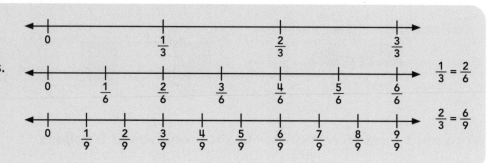

$$\frac{1}{3} = \frac{2}{6}$$

$$\frac{2}{3} = \frac{6}{9}$$

Use each number line to find the equivalent fractions.

1 $\dfrac{1}{2} = \dfrac{\square}{4}$

2 $\dfrac{1}{3} = \dfrac{\square}{6}$

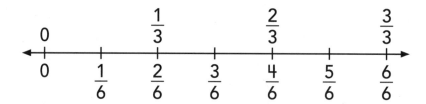

3 $\dfrac{1}{2} = \dfrac{\square}{8}$

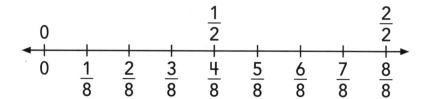

Complete each number line.

4

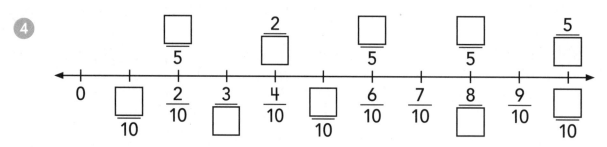

© Scholastic Inc.

Hide and Seek

Color the space in the middle blue. Also color each space with an equivalent fraction for the fraction in the middle blue. Color all the other spaces yellow.

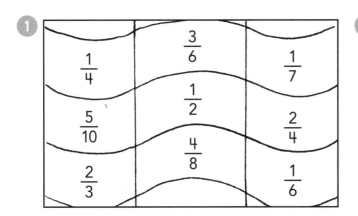

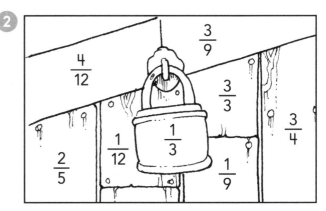

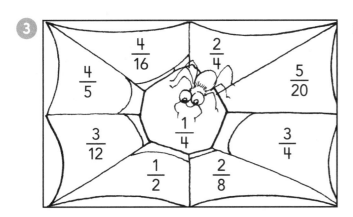

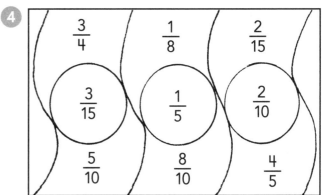

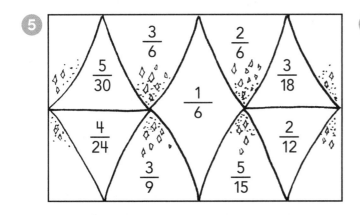

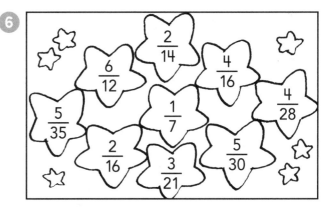

 Jason and his friends are playing hide and seek. Jason finds 5 of the 10 who are hiding right away. What fraction of children are still hiding? Show your work on another sheet of paper. Then, write an equivalent fraction for your answer.

Jasper and Kitty

When determining equivalent fractions, ask yourself these questions:
What factor do I multiply by to equal the new denominator?

$$\frac{1}{3} = \frac{}{12} \qquad\qquad \frac{1}{3} \times \frac{}{\ } = \frac{}{12} \qquad\qquad \frac{1}{3} \times \frac{}{4} = \frac{}{12}$$

Then, multiply the numerator by the same factor to find the equivalent fraction.

$$\frac{1}{3} \times \frac{4}{4} = \frac{}{12} \qquad\qquad \frac{1}{3} \times \frac{1}{3} = \frac{4}{12} \qquad\qquad \frac{1}{3} = \frac{4}{12}$$

Complete the story using each missing numerator for the factor that creates the equivalent fraction.

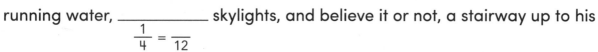

Once upon a time, there was a big puppy named Jasper.

Jasper loved his owners. Jasper never had a desire to run

away because his doghouse was amazing. He had his own

running water, _____ skylights, and believe it or not, a stairway up to his

$$\frac{1}{4} = \frac{}{12}$$

master's tree house. What a view it had! Jasper could see for at least _____

$$\frac{1}{3} = \frac{}{6}$$

miles from the tree house.

From the tree house, Jasper could see so many cats. He would stay in the tree

house for at least _____ hours at a time. Of course, he would spend maybe

$$\frac{2}{3} = \frac{}{12}$$

_____ of those hours sleeping.

$$\frac{1}{2} = \frac{}{10}$$

One day, Jasper saw a cat on a fence making faces at him. This went on for at least _____ minutes. Jasper had had enough. He decided to chase the

$$\frac{3}{5} = \frac{}{10}$$

cat away.

But was the fence too high for Jasper to jump over? He had grown large from

the healthy diet his owners fed him _____ times a day. He stood over

$$\frac{1}{3} = \frac{}{9}$$

_____ feet tall when he placed his front legs on his master's shoulders.

$$\frac{1}{2} = \frac{}{12}$$

The fence was _____ feet high. Jasper was ready to take a chance. Wow,

$$\frac{2}{3} = \frac{}{15}$$

did Jasper leap! He leaped all the way to the other side of the yard! Jasper raced

around the yard for at least _____ minutes because he was so excited about

$$\frac{4}{8} = \frac{}{16}$$

his big leap.

The cat found itself darting back and forth as fast as its _____ short legs

$$\frac{1}{2} = \frac{}{8}$$

would carry it. Jasper did not want to hurt the cat, but he couldn't forget that he had

spent _____ minutes trying to ignore it making faces at him. Jasper chased

$$\frac{3}{4} = \frac{}{8}$$

the cat for what seemed like _____ hours. Finally, they were both so tired,

$$\frac{2}{3} = \frac{}{6}$$

they had to stop. Then, they realized it was fun to chase each other. Jasper and Kitty

decided to meet _____ times a week from then on.

$$\frac{1}{3} = \frac{}{12}$$

On another sheet of paper, finish the story using equivalent fractions
for missing words. Have a friend solve and fill in the blanks.

Let's Get Reducing!

To reduce a faction to lowest terms, find a common factor that will divide into both the numerator and the denominator. In the example below, the factor 2 will work. The factor 4, however, is better. When the only factor is 1, the fraction has been reduced to lowest terms.

$$\frac{4 \div 2}{8 \div 2} = \frac{2}{4}$$

Divide by 2.
Can you divide again? Yes!

$$\frac{2 \div 2}{4 \div 2} = \frac{1}{2}$$

Divide by 2.
Can you divide again? No!

$$\frac{4 \div 4}{8 \div 4} = \frac{1}{2}$$

Divide by 4.
Can you divide again? No!

Choose the greatest common factor for each fraction from the box.
Divide and reduce to lowest terms.

1) $\boxed{3 \quad 2 \atop 4}$ $\dfrac{2 \div \square}{4 \div \square} =$

2) $\boxed{6 \quad 3 \atop 2}$ $\dfrac{6 \div \square}{9 \div \square} =$

3) $\boxed{4 \quad 5 \atop 2}$ $\dfrac{5 \div \square}{10 \div \square} =$

4) $\boxed{3 \quad 5 \atop 2}$ $\dfrac{10 \div \square}{15 \div \square} =$

5) $\boxed{2 \quad 4 \atop 6}$ $\dfrac{4 \div \square}{8 \div \square} =$

6) $\boxed{8 \quad 2 \atop 10}$ $\dfrac{10 \div \square}{12 \div \square} =$

7) $\boxed{2 \quad 8 \atop 3}$ $\dfrac{3 \div \square}{6 \div \square} =$

8) $\boxed{4 \quad 6 \atop 3}$ $\dfrac{3 \div \square}{9 \div \square} =$

9) $\boxed{2 \quad 7 \atop 4}$ $\dfrac{7 \div \square}{14 \div \square} =$

10) $\boxed{2 \quad 3 \atop 6}$ $\dfrac{6 \div \square}{8 \div \square} =$

11) $\boxed{5 \quad 10 \atop 3}$ $\dfrac{5 \div \square}{15 \div \square} =$

12) $\boxed{6 \quad 8 \atop 4}$ $\dfrac{4 \div \square}{16 \div \square} =$

 Maria checked out 9 books at the library. She read 3 of them on the first day. What fraction of the books did she have left to read? Show your work on another sheet of paper. Reduce to lowest terms.

Birds of a Feather

Reduce the fraction on each bird to lowest terms. Then, draw the path to the correct nest.

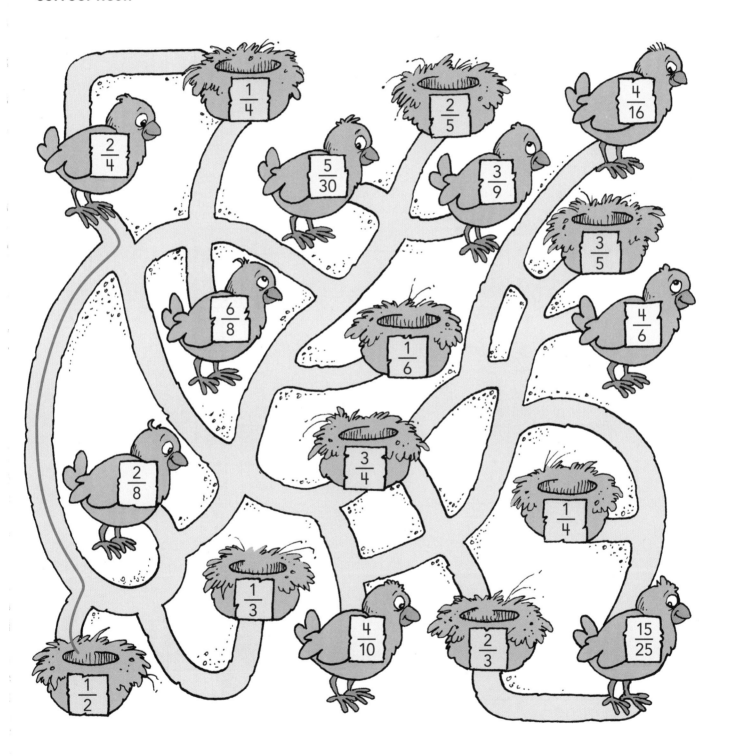

Fraction Action

Write the fraction for each shaded box. Reduce to lowest terms.
Then, draw the reduced fraction in the empty box.

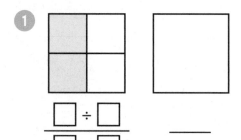

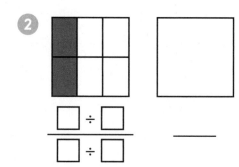

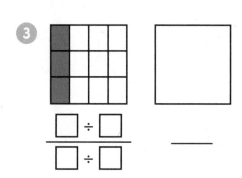

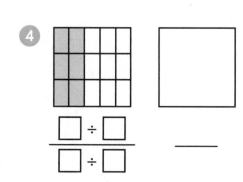

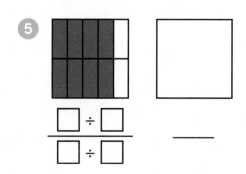

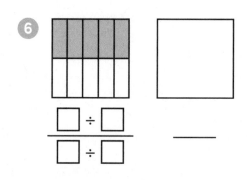

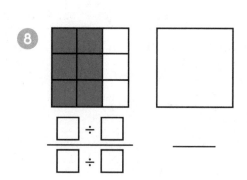

Reducing Riddle

Reduce each fraction to lowest terms.
Then, use the code to answer the riddle below.

O $\dfrac{2}{4} = \dfrac{1}{\rule{1cm}{0.4pt}}$

S $\dfrac{4}{14} = \dfrac{2}{\rule{1cm}{0.4pt}}$

A $\dfrac{10}{15} = \dfrac{2}{\rule{1cm}{0.4pt}}$

B $\dfrac{2}{32} = \dfrac{1}{\rule{1cm}{0.4pt}}$

E $\dfrac{2}{16} = \dfrac{1}{\rule{1cm}{0.4pt}}$

! $\dfrac{2}{12} = \dfrac{1}{\rule{1cm}{0.4pt}}$

T $\dfrac{22}{24} = \dfrac{\rule{1cm}{0.4pt}}{12}$

M $\dfrac{2}{26} = \dfrac{1}{\rule{1cm}{0.4pt}}$

H $\dfrac{4}{10} = \dfrac{2}{\rule{1cm}{0.4pt}}$

D $\dfrac{10}{100} = \dfrac{1}{\rule{1cm}{0.4pt}}$

N $\dfrac{2}{24} = \dfrac{1}{\rule{1cm}{0.4pt}}$

L $\dfrac{2}{18} = \dfrac{1}{\rule{1cm}{0.4pt}}$

Y $\dfrac{2}{28} = \dfrac{1}{\rule{1cm}{0.4pt}}$

P $\dfrac{4}{16} = \dfrac{\rule{1cm}{0.4pt}}{4}$

R $\dfrac{2}{8} = \dfrac{1}{\rule{1cm}{0.4pt}}$

Why was the math teacher crying?

___ ___   ___ ___ ___   ___ ___ ___
5   8   5   3   10   11   2   2

___ ___ ___ ___   ___ ___ ___ ___ ___ ___ ___ ___
13 3 12 14   1   4   2   16 9   8   13 7   6

On another sheet of paper, write a fraction and reduce it to lowest terms. Using a small colored square sheet of paper, cover up one of the numbers on either side of the equation. Have a friend figure out what the covered number is.

Hidden Numbers

To find the fractional part of a whole number, follow these steps.

1. Turn the whole number into a fraction.

$$12 \rightarrow \frac{12}{1}$$

2. Multiply the two fractions.

$$\frac{1}{3} \times \frac{12}{1} = \frac{12}{3}$$

3. Divide the numerator by the denominator.

$$3 \overline{\smash{\big)}\,12} = 4$$

Find the fractional part of each number.

1 $\frac{1}{3}$ of 9 =

2 $\frac{1}{5}$ of 10 =

3 $\frac{1}{4}$ of 20 =

4 $\frac{1}{2}$ of 10 =

5 $\frac{1}{6}$ of 12 =

6 $\frac{1}{7}$ of 14 =

7 $\frac{1}{3}$ of 12 =

8 $\frac{1}{5}$ of 25 =

9 $\frac{1}{3}$ of 6 =

10 $\frac{2}{3}$ of 6 =

11 $\frac{1}{4}$ of 28 =

12 $\frac{1}{5}$ of 30 =

13 $\frac{1}{9}$ of 18 =

14 $\frac{1}{3}$ of 15 =

15 $\frac{1}{4}$ of 16 =

16 $\frac{2}{5}$ of 10 =

What's My Number?

Find the fractional part of each number.

1 $\frac{3}{5}$ of 10 =

2 $\frac{1}{3}$ of 9 =

3 $\frac{3}{4}$ of 12 =

4 $\frac{2}{3}$ of 6 =

5 $\frac{4}{5}$ of 15 =

6 $\frac{2}{3}$ of 15 =

7 $\frac{3}{4}$ of 16 =

8 $\frac{5}{6}$ of 18 =

9 $\frac{4}{7}$ of 21 =

10 $\frac{3}{7}$ of 21 =

11 $\frac{5}{8}$ of 24 =

12 $\frac{3}{5}$ of 20 =

Number Searching

Find the fractional part of each number.

1 $\frac{1}{3}$ of 30 =   **2** $\frac{1}{4}$ of 24 =   **3** $\frac{2}{3}$ of 9 =   **4** $\frac{1}{3}$ of 27 =

5 $\frac{1}{6}$ of 18 =   **6** $\frac{1}{5}$ of 40 =   **7** $\frac{1}{7}$ of 21 =   **8** $\frac{4}{7}$ of 14 =

9 $\frac{2}{9}$ of 18 =   **10** $\frac{3}{4}$ of 16 =   **11** $\frac{1}{8}$ of 56 =   **12** $\frac{1}{3}$ of 33 =

13 $\frac{1}{4}$ of 32 =   **14** $\frac{5}{6}$ of 12 =   **15** $\frac{1}{8}$ of 32 =   **16** $\frac{3}{6}$ of 24 =

17 $\frac{1}{9}$ of 27 =   **18** $\frac{1}{3}$ of 18 =   **19** $\frac{3}{5}$ of 15 =   **20** $\frac{1}{12}$ of 24 =

Can They Be Solved?

Find the fractional part of each number.

A $\dfrac{1}{3}$ of 12 =

B $\dfrac{5}{6}$ of 12 =

C $\dfrac{4}{9}$ of 27 =

D $\dfrac{3}{7}$ of 21 =

Solve each word problem. Write the letter of the problem above in the box whose answer matches the answer to each word problem.

1 Tony had 21 math problems for homework. Four-sevenths of the problems are multiplication problems. How many multiplication problems did Tony have for homework?

2 Carter has 12 marbles. One-third of the marbles are silver. How many silver marbles does Carter have?

3 There are 15 girls in Kristen's scout troop. Three-fifths of the girls went camping last weekend. How many girls went camping?

4 There are 25 students in Mr. Weaver's class. Two-fifths of his students complete their science projects early. How many students complete their projects early?

Space Comparisons

Use the number lines to compare the fractions using >, <, or =.

A number line can be used to compare fractions. The fraction of greatest value is the fraction farthest to the right on the number line. The fraction of least value is the fraction farthest to the left on the number line.

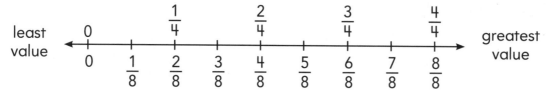

least value $\leftarrow$ 0 $\quad \frac{1}{4} \quad \frac{2}{4} \quad \frac{3}{4} \quad \frac{4}{4}$ $\rightarrow$ greatest value

0 $\quad \frac{1}{8} \quad \frac{2}{8} \quad \frac{3}{8} \quad \frac{4}{8} \quad \frac{5}{8} \quad \frac{6}{8} \quad \frac{7}{8} \quad \frac{8}{8}$

Saturn has over 50 satellites. To learn the name of one of them, write the letter of each number sentence with a < sign in order on the lines.

_____ _____ _____

P $\frac{1}{8} \square \frac{1}{4}$ T $\frac{3}{4} \square \frac{5}{8}$ I $\frac{4}{4} \square \frac{8}{8}$ A $\frac{1}{8} \square \frac{2}{8}$ E $\frac{2}{4} \square \frac{3}{8}$

B $\frac{3}{4} \square \frac{2}{8}$ K $\frac{1}{4} \square \frac{2}{8}$ N $\frac{3}{4} \square \frac{7}{8}$ S $\frac{3}{8} \square \frac{1}{4}$ V $\frac{8}{8} \square \frac{6}{8}$

least value $\leftarrow$ 0 $\quad \frac{1}{5} \quad \frac{2}{5} \quad \frac{3}{5} \quad \frac{4}{5} \quad \frac{5}{5}$ $\rightarrow$ greatest value

0 $\quad \frac{1}{10} \quad \frac{2}{10} \quad \frac{3}{10} \quad \frac{4}{10} \quad \frac{5}{10} \quad \frac{6}{10} \quad \frac{7}{10} \quad \frac{8}{10} \quad \frac{9}{10} \quad \frac{8}{10}$

To learn the name of another satellite of Saturn, write the letter of each number sentence with a > sign in order on the lines.

_____ _____ _____ _____ _____ _____

P $\frac{4}{10} \square \frac{1}{5}$ C $\frac{2}{10} \square \frac{1}{5}$ H $\frac{5}{10} \square \frac{4}{10}$

O $\frac{2}{5} \square \frac{3}{10}$ E $\frac{4}{5} \square \frac{2}{10}$ D $\frac{2}{10} \square \frac{1}{5}$

B $\frac{3}{5} \square \frac{5}{10}$ F $\frac{1}{10} \square \frac{1}{5}$ M $\frac{4}{10} \square \frac{4}{5}$ E $\frac{5}{5} \square \frac{9}{10}$

Who's Greater?

To compare fractions, first look at the denominators. If the denominators are different, find a common denominator to make equivalent fractions.

1. Find a common denominator. 6 is a multiple of both 3 and 6.

$$\frac{2}{3} \square \frac{1}{6}$$

2. Make equivalent fractions.

$$\frac{2 \times 2}{3 \times 2} = \frac{4}{6} \square \frac{1}{6}$$

3. Compare the fractions.

$$\frac{4}{6} \boxed{>} \frac{1}{6}$$

Find a common denominator and make equivalent fractions.
Compare using >, <, or =.

1. $\frac{1}{2} \square \frac{2}{6}$

2. $\frac{4}{5} \square \frac{8}{10}$

3. $\frac{7}{10} \square \frac{9}{10}$

4. $\frac{3}{4} \square \frac{4}{8}$

5. $\frac{1}{10} \square \frac{1}{5}$

6. $\frac{3}{14} \square \frac{3}{7}$

7. $\frac{3}{4} \square \frac{6}{12}$

8. $\frac{3}{6} \square \frac{2}{6}$

9. $\frac{4}{5} \square \frac{3}{10}$

10. $\frac{1}{2} \square \frac{3}{4}$

11. $\frac{3}{4} \square \frac{2}{8}$

12. $\frac{1}{2} \square \frac{2}{4}$

13. $\frac{3}{5} \square \frac{6}{10}$

14. $\frac{2}{3} \square \frac{6}{9}$

15. $\frac{7}{8} \square \frac{4}{8}$

16. $\frac{10}{12} \square \frac{5}{6}$

What's My Size?

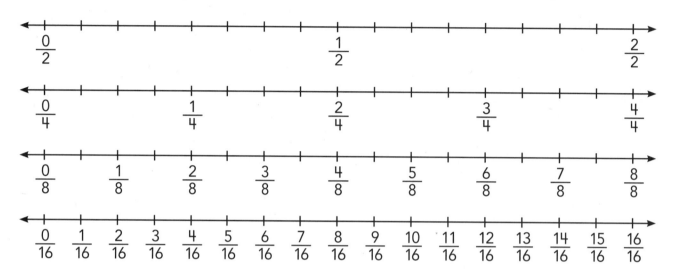

Write each fraction from the Fraction Bank below in the correct column.

less than 1/2	equivalent to 1/2	greater than 1/2

Fraction Bank

$\frac{4}{4}$ $\frac{1}{8}$ $\frac{2}{4}$ $\frac{8}{16}$ $\frac{15}{16}$ $\frac{3}{4}$ $\frac{1}{2}$ $\frac{11}{16}$

$\frac{3}{16}$ $\frac{13}{16}$ $\frac{2}{16}$ $\frac{5}{8}$ $\frac{3}{8}$ $\frac{7}{16}$ $\frac{4}{8}$ $\frac{1}{16}$ $\frac{5}{16}$ $\frac{9}{16}$

 Using 24 as the denominator, write a fraction for each column. Show your work on another sheet of paper.

Compare and Conquer

Compare the fractions using >, <, or =. Then, write the letter of each number sentence with a > sign in order on the lines below to learn the name of an Arctic explorer.

K $\dfrac{1}{4}$ ☐ $\dfrac{1}{2}$ **R** $\dfrac{3}{8}$ ☐ $\dfrac{1}{8}$

O $\dfrac{1}{3}$ ☐ $\dfrac{1}{6}$ **B** $\dfrac{8}{10}$ ☐ $\dfrac{3}{10}$

C $\dfrac{1}{4}$ ☐ $\dfrac{2}{4}$ **E** $\dfrac{2}{3}$ ☐ $\dfrac{1}{3}$

R $\dfrac{5}{6}$ ☐ $\dfrac{2}{6}$ **H** $\dfrac{1}{8}$ ☐ $\dfrac{1}{4}$ **D** $\dfrac{6}{8}$ ☐ $\dfrac{3}{4}$ **T** $\dfrac{5}{6}$ ☐ $\dfrac{2}{6}$

K $\dfrac{1}{4}$ ☐ $\dfrac{6}{8}$ **P** $\dfrac{3}{4}$ ☐ $\dfrac{1}{8}$ **E** $\dfrac{4}{5}$ ☐ $\dfrac{1}{5}$ **A** $\dfrac{2}{3}$ ☐ $\dfrac{1}{6}$

R $\dfrac{6}{8}$ ☐ $\dfrac{1}{16}$ **J** $\dfrac{1}{2}$ ☐ $\dfrac{2}{4}$ **Q** $\dfrac{3}{4}$ ☐ $\dfrac{4}{4}$ **Y** $\dfrac{2}{3}$ ☐ $\dfrac{1}{3}$

___ ___ ___ ___ ___ ___   ___ ___ ___ ___ ___ **is believed to**

have discovered the North Pole.

Line Them Up!

Identify the fraction for each figure. Then, order each set of fractions from least to greatest.

1

Order: _____ _____ _____ _____

2

Order: _____ _____ _____ _____

3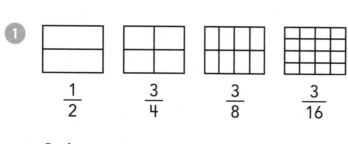

Order: _____ _____ _____

4

Order: _____ _____ _____ _____

Shade each figure to show the fraction.
Then, order each set of fractions from least to greatest.

1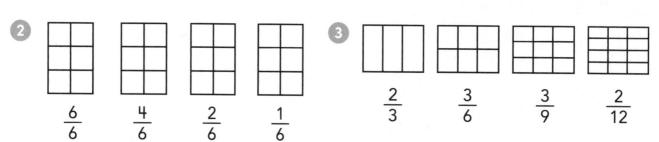

$$\frac{1}{2} \qquad \frac{3}{4} \qquad \frac{3}{8} \qquad \frac{3}{16}$$

Order: _____ _____ _____ _____

2

$$\frac{6}{6} \qquad \frac{4}{6} \qquad \frac{2}{6} \qquad \frac{1}{6}$$

Order: _____ _____ _____ _____

3

$$\frac{2}{3} \qquad \frac{3}{6} \qquad \frac{3}{9} \qquad \frac{2}{12}$$

Order: _____ _____ _____ _____

Order in the Court

Order each set of fractions from least to greatest. Use the number line.

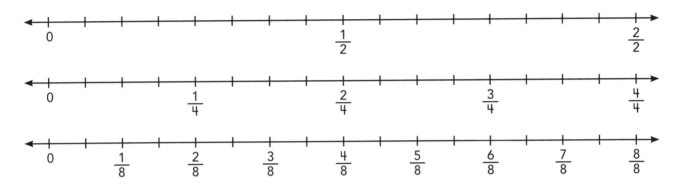

1 $\frac{3}{4}, \frac{1}{8}, \frac{2}{4}, \frac{2}{2}$ _____

2 $\frac{5}{8}, \frac{1}{8}, \frac{1}{2}, \frac{6}{8}$ _____

3 $\frac{3}{8}, \frac{0}{2}, \frac{1}{4}, \frac{6}{8}$ _____

4 $\frac{8}{8}, \frac{3}{4}, \frac{1}{4}, \frac{1}{2}$ _____

5 $\frac{7}{8}, \frac{1}{2}, \frac{1}{8}, \frac{1}{4}$ _____

6 $\frac{8}{8}, \frac{3}{4}, \frac{5}{8}, \frac{1}{2}$ _____

7 $\frac{2}{4}, \frac{7}{8}, \frac{1}{8}, \frac{1}{4}$ _____

8 $\frac{3}{4}, \frac{1}{4}, \frac{5}{8}, \frac{1}{2}$ _____

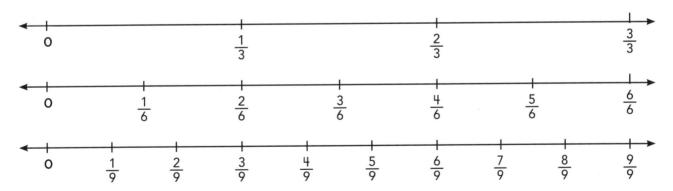

9 $\frac{3}{6}, \frac{3}{3}, \frac{6}{9}, \frac{1}{6}$ _____

10 $\frac{4}{9}, \frac{3}{6}, \frac{2}{3}, \frac{3}{3}$ _____

11 $\frac{8}{9}, \frac{3}{6}, \frac{2}{3}, \frac{1}{9}$ _____

12 $\frac{2}{3}, \frac{5}{6}, \frac{1}{3}, \frac{1}{9}$ _____

Alike Is Good!

When adding fractions with the same denominator, add the numerators.
The denominator does not change. If necessary, reduce to lowest terms.

$$\frac{1}{6} \quad + \quad \frac{2}{6} \quad = \quad \frac{3}{6} \qquad \frac{3}{6} \quad = \quad \frac{1}{2}$$

Add the shaded parts. Reduce to lowest terms.

1

$$\frac{1}{4} + \frac{2}{4} = \underline{\hspace{1.5cm}}$$

2

$$\frac{2}{5} + \frac{2}{5} = \underline{\hspace{1.5cm}}$$

3

$$\frac{1}{6} + \frac{2}{6} = \underline{\hspace{1.5cm}}$$

4

$$\frac{1}{4} + \frac{1}{4} = \underline{\hspace{1.5cm}}$$

5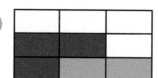

$$\frac{3}{9} + \frac{2}{9} = \underline{\hspace{1.5cm}}$$

6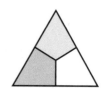

$$\frac{1}{3} + \frac{1}{3} = \underline{\hspace{1.5cm}}$$

7

$$\frac{1}{12} + \frac{1}{12} = \underline{\hspace{1.5cm}}$$

8

$$\frac{1}{2} + \frac{1}{2} = \underline{\hspace{1.5cm}}$$

9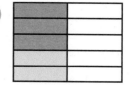

$$\frac{3}{10} + \frac{2}{10} = \underline{\hspace{1.5cm}}$$

 Jake and Sam's mom baked an apple pie for dessert—their favorite! She sliced it into 8 pieces. Jake ate 2/8 of the pie. Sam ate 3/8 of the pie. How much of the pie did they eat altogether. On another sheet of paper, draw a picture to show your answer.

Driving Down Fractions Lane

Add. Reduce to lowest terms.

$\dfrac{1}{6} + \dfrac{4}{6} = $ _____

$\dfrac{3}{8} + \dfrac{1}{8} = $ _____

$\dfrac{4}{9} + \dfrac{3}{9} = $ _____

START HERE

$\dfrac{5}{10} + \dfrac{3}{10} = $ _____

$\dfrac{1}{9} + \dfrac{3}{9} = $ _____

$\dfrac{4}{8} + \dfrac{2}{8} = $ _____

$\dfrac{3}{8} + \dfrac{2}{8} = $ _____

$\dfrac{1}{12} + \dfrac{6}{12} = $ _____

CURVE

$\dfrac{3}{11} + \dfrac{2}{11} = $ _____

$\dfrac{3}{6} + \dfrac{2}{6} = $ _____

$\dfrac{3}{10} + \dfrac{1}{10} = $ _____

$\dfrac{4}{8} + \dfrac{3}{8} = $ _____

$\dfrac{1}{7} + \dfrac{2}{7} = $ _____

$\dfrac{3}{5} + \dfrac{1}{5} = $ _____

$\dfrac{2}{7} + \dfrac{4}{7} = $ _____

$\dfrac{7}{14} + \dfrac{6}{14} = $ _____

$\dfrac{1}{4} + \dfrac{2}{4} = $ _____

$\dfrac{4}{12} + \dfrac{5}{12} = $ _____

STOP

$\dfrac{3}{6} + \dfrac{1}{6} = $ _____

The Proper Way to Add

When the numerator and the denominator are the same, the fraction has a value of 1.

$\dfrac{1}{3} + \dfrac{2}{3} = \dfrac{3}{3} = 1$

When the numerator is equal to or greater than the denominator, the fraction is called an **improper fraction**.

$\dfrac{2}{3}$ + $\dfrac{2}{3}$ = $\dfrac{4}{3}$

$\dfrac{4}{3}$ can be changed to a mixed number by dividing the numerator by the denominator.

$3\overline{\smash{)}4} \begin{array}{r} 1 \\ 4 \\ -3 \\ \hline 1 \end{array}$ $= 1\dfrac{1}{3}$

Add. Change each improper fraction to a mixed number. Reduce to lowest terms.

1. $\dfrac{3}{8} + \dfrac{6}{8} =$ _____

2. $\dfrac{2}{3} + \dfrac{2}{3} =$ _____

3. $\dfrac{3}{6} + \dfrac{5}{6} =$ _____

4. $\dfrac{6}{9} + \dfrac{5}{9} =$ _____

5. $\dfrac{7}{12} + \dfrac{6}{12} =$ _____

6. $\dfrac{7}{8} + \dfrac{2}{8} =$ _____

7. $\dfrac{6}{10} + \dfrac{6}{10} =$ _____

8. $\dfrac{2}{3} + \dfrac{1}{3} =$ _____

9. $\dfrac{4}{11} + \dfrac{9}{11} =$ _____

1. $\dfrac{1}{4}$
$+ \dfrac{3}{4}$

2. $\dfrac{3}{5}$
$+ \dfrac{4}{5}$

3. $\dfrac{3}{7}$
$+ \dfrac{5}{7}$

4. $\dfrac{3}{8}$
$+ \dfrac{7}{8}$

5. $\dfrac{5}{8}$
$+ \dfrac{6}{8}$

6. $\dfrac{8}{12}$
$+ \dfrac{7}{12}$

7. $\dfrac{3}{4}$
$+ \dfrac{2}{4}$

8. $\dfrac{6}{9}$
$+ \dfrac{6}{9}$

9. $\dfrac{6}{10}$
$+ \dfrac{4}{10}$

10. $\dfrac{3}{9}$
$+ \dfrac{8}{9}$

Is It Proper Yet?

When the numerator and the denominator are the same number, the fraction has a value of 1. When the numerator is equal to, or greater than the denominator, the fraction is called an **improper fraction**. When a number has two parts, a whole number and a fraction, it is called a **mixed number**.

$\frac{9}{7}$ can be changed to a mixed number by dividing the numerator by the denominator.

$$7 \overline{)9} = 1\frac{2}{7}$$
$$\underline{-7}$$
$$2$$

Write a whole number for the fractions below each box.

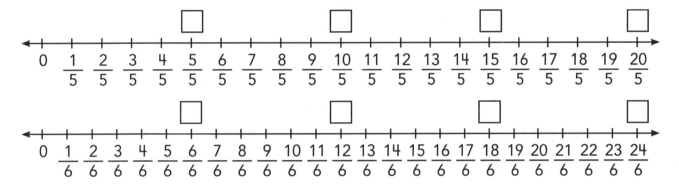

Change each fraction to a whole or a mixed number.

1. $\frac{10}{2} =$ _____ $\frac{10}{7} =$ _____ $\frac{8}{5} =$ _____ $\frac{7}{6} =$ _____ $\frac{5}{4} =$ _____

2. $\frac{13}{2} =$ _____ $\frac{17}{5} =$ _____ $\frac{13}{3} =$ _____ $\frac{24}{6} =$ _____ $\frac{18}{9} =$ _____

3. $\frac{15}{7} =$ _____ $\frac{36}{12} =$ _____ $\frac{12}{4} =$ _____ $\frac{12}{3} =$ _____ $\frac{25}{5} =$ _____

4. $\frac{17}{3} =$ _____ $\frac{15}{4} =$ _____ $\frac{13}{6} =$ _____ $\frac{9}{3} =$ _____ $\frac{13}{5} =$ _____

5. $\frac{8}{7} =$ _____ $\frac{17}{8} =$ _____ $\frac{21}{5} =$ _____ $\frac{21}{7} =$ _____ $\frac{20}{3} =$ _____

Keep on Adding

**Add. Change each improper fraction to a mixed number. Reduce to lowest terms.
Then, use the code to answer the question below.**

(A) $\dfrac{2}{5} + \dfrac{2}{5} =$ _____

(S) $\dfrac{1}{8} + \dfrac{7}{8} =$ _____

(C) $\dfrac{3}{4} + \dfrac{2}{4} =$ _____

(T) $\dfrac{3}{7} + \dfrac{2}{7} =$ _____

(P) $\dfrac{2}{5} + \dfrac{4}{5} =$ _____

(W) $\dfrac{8}{9} + \dfrac{10}{9} =$ _____

(I) $\dfrac{3}{6} + \dfrac{2}{6} =$ _____

(X) $\dfrac{4}{7} + \dfrac{6}{7} =$ _____

(B) $\dfrac{5}{6} + \dfrac{4}{6} =$ _____

(Y) $\dfrac{5}{12} + \dfrac{3}{12} =$ _____

(T) $\dfrac{8}{10} + \dfrac{6}{10} =$ _____

(E) $\dfrac{3}{9} + \dfrac{1}{9} =$ _____

(N) $\dfrac{8}{11} + \dfrac{5}{11} =$ _____

(K) $\dfrac{3}{10} + \dfrac{2}{10} =$ _____

(O) $\dfrac{4}{8} + \dfrac{6}{8} =$ _____

How long is a marathon race?

It is over _____ _____ _____ _____ _____ _____ –

$1\dfrac{2}{5}$ 2 $\dfrac{4}{9}$ $1\dfrac{2}{11}$ $\dfrac{5}{7}$ $\dfrac{2}{3}$

_____ _____ _____ **miles long!**

1 $\dfrac{5}{6}$ $1\dfrac{3}{7}$

Creating Mixed Numbers

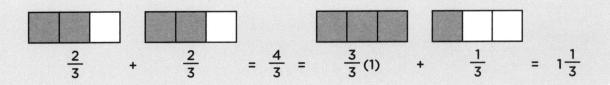

$$\frac{2}{3} \quad + \quad \frac{2}{3} \quad = \frac{4}{3} = \quad \frac{3}{3}(1) \quad + \quad \frac{1}{3} \quad = 1\frac{1}{3}$$

Add. Change to a mixed number. Reduce to lowest terms.

1

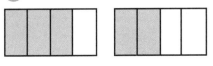

___ + ___ = ___ =

2

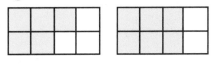

___ + ___ = ___ =

3

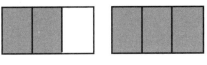

___ + ___ = ___ =

4

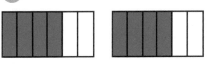

___ + ___ = ___ =

5

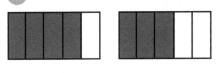

___ + ___ = ___ =

6

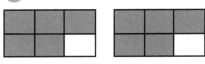

___ + ___ = ___ =

7

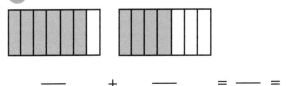

___ + ___ = ___ =

8

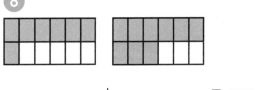

___ + ___ = ___ =

9

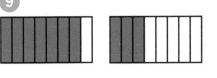

___ + ___ = ___ =

10

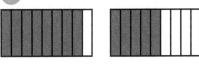

___ + ___ = ___ =

Fraction Subtraction

How many squares are there in all? 12

What fraction are shaded? $\frac{6}{12}$

Subtract the fraction of marked-out squares. $\frac{6}{12} - \frac{3}{12} = \frac{3}{12}$

What fraction of shaded squares remain unmarked? $\frac{3}{12} = \frac{1}{4}$

Write out the fraction subtraction problem. Subtract. Reduce to lowest terms.

1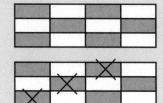
$$\frac{4}{10}$$
$$-\frac{1}{10}$$

2 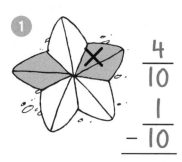 ___

3 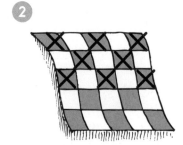 ___

4 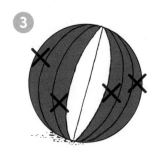 ___

5 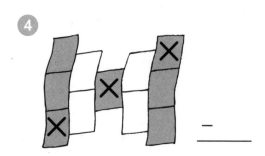 ___

6  ___

7  ___

Mr. Fraction, Take It Away!

When subtracting fractions with same denominators, subtract the numerators. The denominator does not change.

Subtract. Reduce to lowest terms.

1

$\frac{8}{9}$
$- \frac{4}{9}$

$\frac{7}{10}$
$- \frac{3}{10}$

$\frac{4}{12}$
$- \frac{1}{12}$

$\frac{5}{9}$
$- \frac{3}{9}$

$\frac{6}{7}$
$- \frac{6}{7}$

2

$\frac{6}{8}$
$- \frac{4}{8}$

$\frac{13}{14}$
$- \frac{7}{14}$

$\frac{9}{20}$
$- \frac{4}{20}$

$\frac{6}{9}$
$- \frac{3}{9}$

$\frac{6}{12}$
$- \frac{4}{12}$

3

$\frac{17}{20}$
$- \frac{9}{20}$

$\frac{7}{15}$
$- \frac{3}{15}$

$\frac{15}{16}$
$- \frac{9}{16}$

$\frac{3}{4}$
$- \frac{1}{4}$

$\frac{11}{15}$
$- \frac{9}{15}$

FRACTIONS TAKE 1

What a Story!

Solve each problem.

1 Cindy and A. J. discovered a pizza box on the counter! In the box, 7/8 of the pizza remained. They each took a piece. What fraction of the pizza now remained?

2 Heather and Roger inflated a total of 20 balloons for the birthday party. There were 12 blue balloons. The rest of the balloons were other colors. Roger gave away 3 blue balloons. What fraction of the blue balloons remained?

3 Joe and Eva went to the carnival on Saturday. They had waited all week to submerge Dad in the dunk tank! Together they bought 10 balls to throw. Joe threw 4/10 of the balls. Eva threw 3/10 of the balls. What fraction of the balls did they throw?

4 On "Hat Day" 12 students walked into class wearing hats. 5/12 of the hats were huge. The rest were normal size. Students wearing the huge hats were asked to remove them so that the students behind them could see the board. What fraction of the students did not remove their hats during class?

5 Bill and Dave went to the park. They brought with them 32 ounces of delicious ice water. They drank 16 ounces in the first hour. Then, they drank 12 ounces in the second hour. What fraction of the water did they drink?

6 Gwen and Cheryl made a total of 15 cups of lemonade to sell at their corner stand. They sold 7/15 of the cups in the first half hour and 5/15 in the second half hour. What fraction of their drinks did they sell?

Fraction Frenzy

Subtract. Shade all shapes that are equal to 1/2 yellow and all other shapes blue
to find out the answer to the question.

**What is the most
fun subject in the
entire world?**

Let the Fun Begin!

To add fractions when the
denominators are different,
find equivalent fractions
with common denominators.
Then, add.

$$\frac{1}{2}$$

$$\frac{1 \times 2}{2 \times 2} = \frac{2}{4}$$

$$+ \frac{1}{4}$$

$$+ \frac{1}{4}$$

$$\frac{2}{4}$$

$$+ \frac{1}{4}$$

$$\frac{3}{4}$$

Find equivalent fractions with common denominators. Add. Reduce to lowest terms.

1

$$\frac{1}{4}$$
$$+ \frac{1}{8} \quad + \underline{\quad}$$

$$\frac{1}{3}$$
$$+ \frac{1}{9} \quad + \underline{\quad}$$

$$\frac{1}{5}$$
$$+ \frac{1}{10} \quad + \underline{\quad}$$

$$\frac{1}{8}$$
$$+ \frac{1}{16} \quad + \underline{\quad}$$

2

$$\frac{1}{4}$$
$$+ \frac{1}{12} \quad + \underline{\quad}$$

$$\frac{1}{2}$$
$$+ \frac{1}{8} \quad + \underline{\quad}$$

$$\frac{1}{5}$$
$$+ \frac{1}{15} \quad + \underline{\quad}$$

$$\frac{1}{2}$$
$$+ \frac{1}{10} \quad + \underline{\quad}$$

3

$$\frac{1}{3}$$
$$+ \frac{1}{6} \quad + \underline{\quad}$$

$$\frac{1}{4}$$
$$+ \frac{1}{16} \quad + \underline{\quad}$$

$$\frac{1}{3}$$
$$+ \frac{1}{12} \quad + \underline{\quad}$$

$$\frac{1}{2}$$
$$+ \frac{1}{12} \quad + \underline{\quad}$$

 During recess, 2/3 of the students in Ms. McCabe's class played soccer, and 1/6 of the students played basketball. What fraction of the class played soccer and basketball? Show your work on another sheet of paper.

Planet Fractions

Add. Reduce to lowest terms.

$$\frac{2}{7}$$
$$+ \frac{4}{14}$$

$$\frac{1}{9}$$
$$+ \frac{3}{18}$$

$$\frac{1}{8}$$
$$\frac{3}{16}$$
and
$$\frac{1}{3}$$
$$+ \frac{1}{15}$$

$$\frac{2}{5}$$
$$+ \frac{3}{15}$$

$$\frac{2}{5}$$
$$+ \frac{1}{10}$$

$$\frac{1}{3}$$
$$+ \frac{2}{9}$$

$$\frac{1}{6}$$
$$+ \frac{2}{12}$$

$$\frac{1}{4}$$
$$+ \frac{2}{8}$$

$$\frac{3}{7}$$
$$+ \frac{2}{14}$$

$$\frac{1}{2}$$
$$+ \frac{2}{10}$$

$$\frac{1}{4}$$
$$+ \frac{3}{12}$$

$$\frac{4}{5}$$
$$+ \frac{1}{10}$$

$$\frac{1}{5}$$
$$+ \frac{6}{10}$$

$$\frac{1}{3}$$
$$+ \frac{3}{6}$$

Forks in the Road

Add each circled fraction to the fraction at each fork in the road. Find a common denominator. Reduce to lowest terms. Two of the roads will have the same answers. Follow the other road to find the correct path.

$\frac{2}{6}$

$\frac{2}{6} + \frac{1}{2} = \frac{2}{6} + \frac{3}{6} = \left(\frac{5}{6}\right)$ $\frac{2}{6} + \frac{1}{3} = \frac{2}{6} + \frac{2}{6} = \frac{4}{6} = \left(\frac{2}{3}\right)$

$\frac{4}{12}$

$\frac{1}{2}$

$\frac{1}{3}$

$\frac{4}{18}$

$\frac{2}{12}$

$\frac{1}{4}$

$\frac{1}{6}$

$\frac{4}{36}$

$\frac{4}{24}$

A Good Finish

Add the fractions. Then, use the code to answer the question below.
Do not forget to reduce to lowest terms.

Y $\dfrac{1}{2} + \dfrac{1}{6} =$	**O** $\dfrac{1}{4} + \dfrac{2}{12} =$	**S** $\dfrac{1}{3} + \dfrac{7}{12} =$
U $\dfrac{1}{4} + \dfrac{3}{8} =$	**G** $\dfrac{1}{3} + \dfrac{2}{12} =$	**A** $\dfrac{1}{3} + \dfrac{1}{9} =$
L $\dfrac{2}{3} + \dfrac{1}{12} =$	**T** $\dfrac{1}{4} + \dfrac{1}{8} =$	**W** $\dfrac{1}{6} + \dfrac{1}{12} =$
F $\dfrac{1}{3} + \dfrac{2}{9} =$	**M** $\dfrac{2}{4} + \dfrac{4}{12} =$	**E** $\dfrac{3}{5} + \dfrac{1}{10} =$
N $\dfrac{1}{5} + \dfrac{1}{10} =$	**R** $\dfrac{3}{6} + \dfrac{1}{12} =$	**!** $\dfrac{1}{4} + \dfrac{1}{12} =$
H $\dfrac{1}{2} + \dfrac{3}{8} =$	**D** $\dfrac{1}{5} + \dfrac{1}{15} =$	**I** $\dfrac{1}{5} + \dfrac{2}{10} =$

Why is adding fractions such a blast?

$\dfrac{2}{3}$ $\dfrac{5}{12}$ $\dfrac{5}{8}$ $\quad$ $\dfrac{4}{9}$ $\dfrac{3}{4}$ $\dfrac{1}{4}$ $\dfrac{4}{9}$ $\dfrac{2}{3}$ $\dfrac{11}{12}$

$\dfrac{5}{9}$ $\dfrac{2}{5}$ $\dfrac{3}{10}$ $\dfrac{2}{5}$ $\dfrac{11}{12}$ $\dfrac{7}{8}$ $\quad$ $\dfrac{5}{12}$ $\dfrac{3}{10}$

$\dfrac{1}{2}$ $\dfrac{5}{12}$ $\dfrac{5}{12}$ $\dfrac{4}{15}$ $\quad$ $\dfrac{3}{8}$ $\dfrac{7}{10}$ $\dfrac{7}{12}$ $\dfrac{5}{6}$ $\dfrac{11}{12}$ $\dfrac{1}{3}$

Geometric Fractions

Check the problems in each space. If the difference is correct, color the shape yellow. If the difference is incorrect, color the shape red.

When subtracting fractions with unlike denominators, find a common denominator and make equivalent fractions. Subtract. Reduce to lowest terms.

$$\frac{1}{2} - \frac{1}{8} = \frac{3}{8}$$

$$\frac{3}{5} - \frac{1}{10} = \frac{1}{2}$$

$$\frac{1}{3} - \frac{1}{6} = \frac{1}{3}$$

$$\frac{3}{4} - \frac{1}{2} = \frac{1}{4}$$

$$\frac{7}{10} - \frac{3}{5} = \frac{1}{10}$$

$$\frac{7}{12} - \frac{1}{3} = \frac{2}{3}$$

$$\frac{6}{10} - \frac{1}{2} = \frac{1}{10}$$

$$\frac{7}{10} - \frac{2}{5} = \frac{3}{10}$$

$$\frac{6}{10} - \frac{1}{5} = \frac{1}{2}$$

$$\frac{7}{8} - \frac{1}{4} = \frac{5}{8}$$

$$\frac{3}{6} - \frac{1}{2} = \frac{1}{2}$$

$$\frac{1}{3} - \frac{1}{9} = \frac{2}{9}$$

$$\frac{1}{3} - \frac{1}{12} = \frac{1}{4}$$

$$\frac{7}{9} - \frac{2}{3} = \frac{1}{2}$$

$$\frac{3}{6} - \frac{1}{3} = \frac{1}{6}$$

$$\frac{4}{6} - \frac{1}{3} = \frac{1}{2}$$

$$\frac{7}{9} - \frac{2}{3} = \frac{1}{2}$$

$$\frac{5}{6} - \frac{2}{3} = \frac{1}{6}$$

$$\frac{3}{5} - \frac{1}{10} = \frac{1}{5}$$

$$\frac{1}{4} - \frac{1}{8} = \frac{1}{8}$$

$$\frac{4}{5} - \frac{2}{10} = \frac{3}{5}$$

$$\frac{4}{5} - \frac{1}{10} = \frac{1}{2}$$

$$\frac{5}{10} - \frac{1}{5} = \frac{3}{10}$$

$$\frac{8}{12} - \frac{1}{3} = \frac{2}{3}$$

$$\frac{5}{9} - \frac{1}{3} = \frac{2}{9}$$

$$\frac{5}{6} - \frac{1}{2} = \frac{1}{3}$$

$$\frac{3}{4} - \frac{1}{2} = \frac{1}{2}$$

$$\frac{1}{2} - \frac{1}{6} = \frac{1}{3}$$

$$\frac{5}{8} - \frac{1}{4} = \frac{3}{8}$$

$$\frac{6}{10} - \frac{2}{5} = \frac{1}{10}$$

$$\frac{1}{2} - \frac{1}{6} = \frac{1}{3}$$

$$\frac{3}{5} - \frac{1}{10} = \frac{1}{2}$$

Fraction Puzzle

**Subtract. Reduce to lowest terms. Write the difference in the puzzle.
Do not forget the hyphens.**

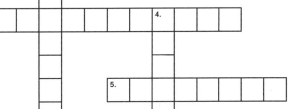
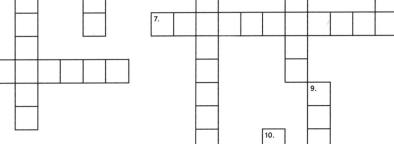
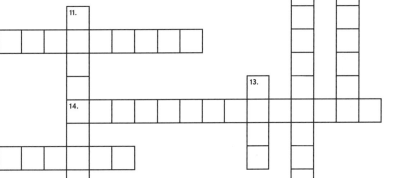

Across

3. $\dfrac{4}{5} - \dfrac{2}{10} = $ _____

5. $\dfrac{5}{6} - \dfrac{1}{3} = $ _____

7. $\dfrac{9}{12} - \dfrac{4}{6} = $ _____

8. $\dfrac{1}{2} - \dfrac{1}{6} = $ _____

12. $\dfrac{7}{9} - \dfrac{1}{3} = $ _____

14. $\dfrac{2}{3} - \dfrac{1}{12} = $ _____

15. $\dfrac{8}{12} - \dfrac{2}{4} = $ _____

Down

1. $\dfrac{6}{8} - \dfrac{2}{4} = $ _____

2. $\dfrac{1}{2} - \dfrac{1}{4} = $ _____   **6.** $\dfrac{2}{8} - \dfrac{1}{4} = $ _____   **10.** $\dfrac{4}{5} - \dfrac{4}{10} = $ _____

3. $\dfrac{7}{10} - \dfrac{2}{5} = $ _____   **8.** $\dfrac{7}{10} - \dfrac{1}{2} = $ _____   **11.** $\dfrac{1}{3} - \dfrac{1}{6} = $ _____

4. $\dfrac{9}{12} - \dfrac{2}{6} = $ _____   **9.** $\dfrac{9}{10} - \dfrac{4}{5} = $ _____   **13.** $\dfrac{6}{8} - \dfrac{3}{4} = $ _____

The Search for the Difference

Subtract. Reduce to lowest terms. Find each answer in the puzzle. The answers will go up, down, forward, backward, and diagonally.

1 $\dfrac{1}{3}$
  $-\dfrac{1}{12}$

2 $\dfrac{1}{4}$
  $-\dfrac{1}{16}$

3 $\dfrac{3}{4}$
  $-\dfrac{2}{8}$

4 $\dfrac{6}{8}$
  $-\dfrac{1}{16}$

5 $\dfrac{2}{6}$
  $-\dfrac{1}{12}$

6 $\dfrac{5}{10}$
  $-\dfrac{1}{2}$

7 $\dfrac{5}{6}$
  $-\dfrac{1}{3}$

8 $\dfrac{5}{6}$
  $-\dfrac{1}{2}$

9 $\dfrac{1}{2}$
  $-\dfrac{3}{10}$

10 $\dfrac{3}{8}$
  $-\dfrac{4}{16}$

11 $\dfrac{6}{9}$
  $-\dfrac{2}{3}$

12 $\dfrac{4}{6}$
  $-\dfrac{1}{3}$

13 $\dfrac{3}{8}$
  $-\dfrac{2}{16}$

14 $\dfrac{4}{5}$
  $-\dfrac{7}{10}$

15 $\dfrac{6}{10}$
  $-\dfrac{2}{5}$

```
O  W  O  N  E  -  F  O  U  R  T  H  H  F  T  E  C  O  E  I
N  N  Z  R  P  U  Q  O  X  -  P  H  N  O  P  Q  O  N  D  U
E  L  E  V  E  N  -  S  I  X  T  E  E  N  T  H  S  E  R  D
-  S  R  E  R  O  N  E  -  H  A  L  F  Q  D  F  I  -  I  R
F  L  O  U  B  F  N  J  G  S  X  M  Y  T  L  R  I  F  H  I
O  B  O  N  E  -  F  I  F  T  H  -  R  A  T  D  N  O  T  H
U  T  H  N  O  N  E  -  T  E  N  T  H  T  Z  H  E  U  -  T
R  T  K  O  W  -  I  G  H  N  J  -  D  Y  R  L  D  R  E  -
T  H  R  E  E  -  S  I  X  T  E  E  N  T  H  S  U  T  N  E
H  E  -  N  -  H  K  H  -  N  K  M  D  V  V  -  J  H  O  N
Z  S  O  V  O  B  N  L  O  C  A  H  T  F  I  F  -  E  N  O
```

Full-Twisting Fun

Follow the course and solve each problem. Reduce to lowest terms.

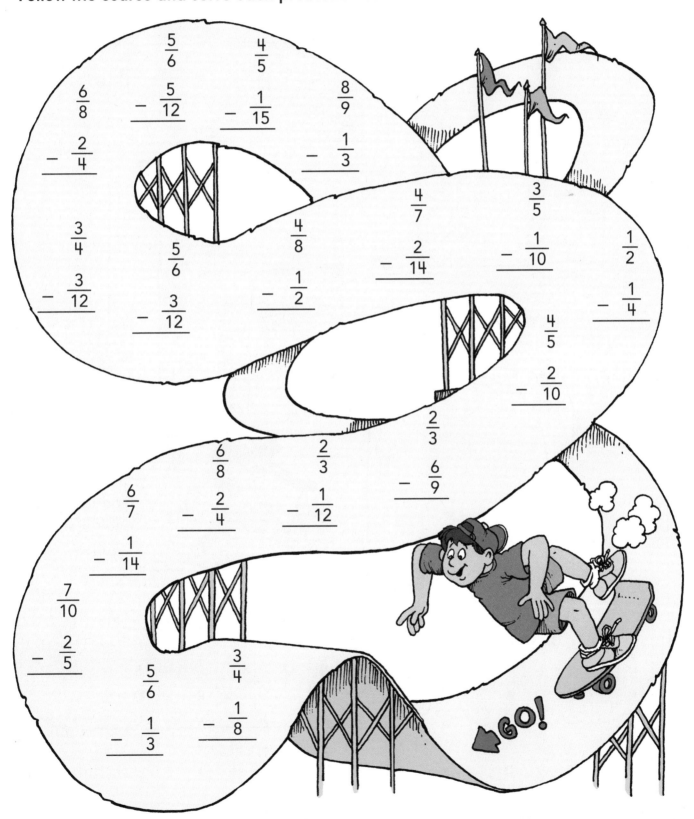

$$\frac{5}{6} - \frac{5}{12}$$

$$\frac{4}{5} - \frac{1}{15}$$

$$\frac{6}{8} - \frac{2}{4}$$

$$\frac{8}{9} - \frac{1}{3}$$

$$\frac{3}{4} - \frac{3}{12}$$

$$\frac{5}{6} - \frac{3}{12}$$

$$\frac{4}{8} - \frac{1}{2}$$

$$\frac{4}{7} - \frac{2}{14}$$

$$\frac{3}{5} - \frac{1}{10}$$

$$\frac{1}{2} - \frac{1}{4}$$

$$\frac{4}{5} - \frac{2}{10}$$

$$\frac{2}{3} - \frac{6}{9}$$

$$\frac{6}{8} - \frac{2}{4}$$

$$\frac{2}{3} - \frac{1}{12}$$

$$\frac{6}{7} - \frac{1}{14}$$

$$\frac{7}{10} - \frac{2}{5}$$

$$\frac{5}{6} - \frac{1}{3}$$

$$\frac{3}{4} - \frac{1}{8}$$

GO!

The Ultimate Challenge Course

Follow the course from start to finish.

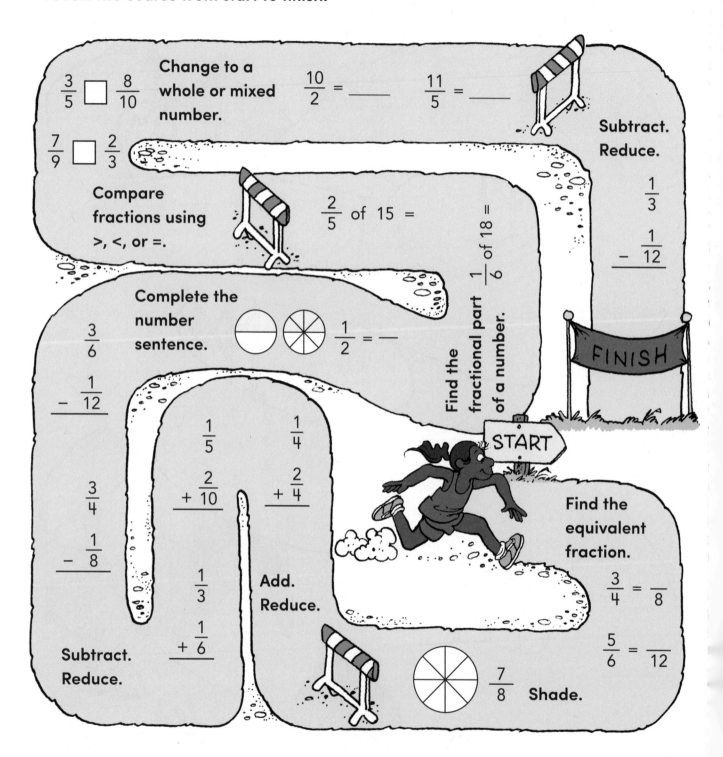

$\dfrac{3}{5}$ ☐ $\dfrac{8}{10}$

Change to a whole or mixed number.

$\dfrac{10}{2} =$ _____ $\dfrac{11}{5} =$ _____

$\dfrac{7}{9}$ ☐ $\dfrac{2}{3}$

Subtract. Reduce.

$\dfrac{1}{3}$
$-\dfrac{1}{12}$

Compare fractions using >, <, or =.

$\dfrac{2}{5}$ of 15 =

Find the fractional part $\dfrac{1}{6}$ of 18 = of a number.

Complete the number sentence.

$\dfrac{1}{2} = \underline{}$

$\dfrac{3}{6}$
$-\dfrac{1}{12}$

$\dfrac{1}{5}$
$+\dfrac{2}{10}$

$\dfrac{1}{4}$
$+\dfrac{2}{4}$

START

$\dfrac{3}{4}$
$-\dfrac{1}{8}$

$\dfrac{1}{3}$
$+\dfrac{1}{6}$

Add. Reduce.

Find the equivalent fraction.

$\dfrac{3}{4} = \dfrac{}{8}$

Subtract. Reduce.

$\dfrac{7}{8}$ Shade.

$\dfrac{5}{6} = \dfrac{}{12}$

FINISH

ANSWER KEY

Page 5
1. 1/4, 2/4, 1/2, 3/8
2. 5/6, 4/8, 4/8, 4/10
3. 1/5, 2/4, 2/6, 4/12
4. 1/3, 5/9, 6/12

Page 6
Check students' shading.

Page 7
1. 4/10 **2.** 5/8 **3.** 6/11 **4.** 1/4
5. 1/2 **6.** 2/12

Page 8
Check students' shading.

Page 9
1. 2 **2.** 2 **3.** 2 **4.** 3 **5.** 2 **6.** 4 **7.** 8 **8.** 5
9. 1/2 = 6/12 **10.** 1/3 = 2/6
11. 1/6 = 3/18 **12.** 1/2 = 3/6

Page 10
1. 2/4 **2.** 2/6 **3.** 4/8
4. 1/5, 2/5, 3/5, 4/5, 5/5,
1/10, 3/10, 5/10, 8/10, 10/10

Page 11
The following should be blue:
1. 3/6, 5/10, 2/4, 4/8, 1/2
2. 4/12, 3/9, 1/3 **3.** 4/16, 3/12, 2/8,
5/20, 1/4 **4.** 3/15, 1/5, 2/10
5. 5/30, 3/18, 4/24, 2/12
6. 2/14, 5/35, 4/28, 3/21, 1/7
Extra Activity: 1/2 children are still
playing, 5/10 = 1/2

Pages 12–13
3, 2, 8, 5, 6, 3, 6, 10, 8, 4, 6, 4, 4

Page 14
1. 2, 1/2 **2.** 3, 2/3 **3.** 5, 1/2 **4.** 5, 2/3
5. 4, 1/2 **6.** 2, 5/6 **7.** 3, 1/2 **8.** 3, 1/3
9. 7, 1/2 **10.** 2, 3/4 **11.** 5, 1/3 **12.** 4, 1/4
Extra Activity: 6/9 = 2/3 of the books

Page 15

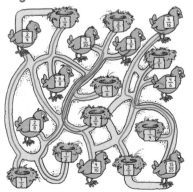

Page 16
1. 2/4 ÷ 2/2 = 1/2 **2.** 2/6 ÷ 2/2 = 1/3
3. 3/12 ÷ 3/3 = 1/4 **4.** 6/15 ÷ 3/3 = 2/5
5. 8/10 ÷ 2/2 = 4/5 **6.** 5/10 ÷ 5/5 = 1/2
7. 7/14 ÷ 7/7 = 1/2 **8.** 6/9 ÷ 3/3 = 2/3
Check students' drawings.

Page 17
O. 2 **S.** 7 **A.** 3 **B.** 16 **E.** 8 **!** 6
T. 11 **M.** 13 **H.** 5 **D.** 10 **N.** 12
L. 9 **Y.** 14 **P.** 1 **R.** 4

HE HAD TOO MANY PROBLEMS!

Page 18
1. 3 **2.** 2 **3.** 5 **4.** 5
5. 2 **6.** 2 **7.** 4 **8.** 5
9. 2 **10.** 4 **11.** 7 **12.** 6
13. 2 **14.** 5 **15.** 4 **16.** 4

Page 19
1. 6 **2.** 3 **3.** 9 **4.** 4 **5.** 12 **6.** 10
7. 12 **8.** 15 **9.** 12 **10.** 9 **11.** 15 **12.** 12

Page 20
1. 10 **2.** 6 **3.** 6 **4.** 9
5. 3 **6.** 8 **7.** 3 **8.** 8
9. 4 **10.** 12 **11.** 7 **12.** 11
13. 8 **14.** 10 **15.** 4 **16.** 12
17. 3 **18.** 6 **19.** 9 **20.** 2

Page 21
A. 4 **B.** 10 **C.** 12 **D.** 9
1. C **2.** A **3.** D **4.** B

Page 22
PAN P. < **T.** > **I.** = **A.** < **E.** >
B. > **K.** = **N.** < **S.** > **V.** >
PHOEBE P. > **C.** = **H.** > **O.** >
E. > **D.** = **B.** > **F.** < **M.** < **E.** >

Page 23
1. > **2.** = **3.** < **4.** > **5.** < **6.** <
7. > **8.** > **9.** > **10.** < **11.** > **12.** =
13. = **14.** = **15.** > **16.** =

Page 24
Less than 1/2: 3/16, 1/8, 2/16, 3/8,
7/16, 1/16, 5/16
1/2 or equivalent: 2/4, 8/16, 1/2, 4/8
Greater than 1/2: 4/4, 15/16, 3/4, 11/16,
13/16, 5/8, 9/16

Page 25
K. < **R.** > **O.** > **B.** > **C.** < **E.** >
R. > **H.** < **D.** = **T.** > **K.** < **P.** >
E. > **A.** > **R.** > **J.** = **Q.** < **Y.** >
ROBERT PEARY

Page 26
1. 1/2, 1/4, 1/3, 1/5,
Order: 1/5, 1/4, 1/3, 1/2
2. 1/16, 1/4, 1/8, 1/2,
Order: 1/16, 1/8, 1/4, 1/2
3. 1/3, 1/2, 1/6, Order: 1/6, 1/3, 1/2
4. 1/6, 1/3, 1/12, 1/9,
Order: 1/12, 1/9, 1/6, 1/3
1. Order: 3/16, 3/8, 1/2, 3/4
2. Order: 1/6, 2/6, 4/6, 6/6
3. Order: 2/12, 3/9, 3/6, 2/3
Check students' shading.

Page 27
1. 1/8, 2/4, 3/4, 2/2 **2.** 1/8, 1/2, 5/8, 6/8
3. 0/2, 1/4, 3/8, 6/8 **4.** 1/4, 1/2, 3/4, 8/8
5. 1/8, 1/4, 1/2, 7/8 **6.** 1/2, 5/8, 3/4, 8/8
7. 1/8, 1/4, 2/4, 7/8 **8.** 1/4, 1/2, 5/8, 3/4
9. 1/6, 3/6, 6/9, 3/3 **10.** 4/9, 3/6, 2/3, 3/3
11. 1/9, 3/6, 2/3, 8/9 **12.** 1/9, 1/3, 2/3, 5/6

Page 28
1. 3/4 **2.** 4/5 **3.** 3/6 = 1/2 **4.** 2/4 = 1/2
5. 5/9 **6.** 2/3 **7.** 2/12 = 1/6 **8.** 2/2 = 1
9. 5/10 = 1/2
Extra Activity: 5/8 of the pie

Page 29

Page 30
1. 9/8 = 1⅛ **2.** 4/3 = 1⅓
3. 8/6 = 1²/₆ = 1⅓ **4.** 11/9 = 1²/₉
5. 13/12 = 1¹/₁₂ **6.** 9/8 = 1⅛
7. 12/10 = 1²/₁₀ = 1⅕ **8.** 3/3 = 1
9. 13/11 = 1²/₁₁
1. 4/4 = 1 **2.** 7/5 = 1²/₅ **3.** 8/7 = 1¹/₇
4. 10/8 = 1²/₈ = 1¼ **5.** 11/8 = 1³/₈
6. 15/12 = 1³/₁₂ = 1¼ **7.** 5/4 = 1¼
8. 12/9 = 1³/₉ = 1⅓ **9.** 10/10 = 1
10. 11/9 = 1²/₉

Page 31

1, 2, 3, 4; 1, 2, 3, 4
1. 5, 1³/₇, 1³/₅, 1¹/₆, 1¹/₄ **2.** 6¹/₂, 3²/₅, 4¹/₃, 4, 2
3. 2¹/₇, 3, 3, 4, 5 **4.** 5²/₃, 3³/₄, 2¹/₆, 3, 2³/₅
5. 1¹/₇, 2¹/₈, 4¹/₅, 3, 6²/₃

Page 32

A. 4/5 **S.** 1 **C.** 1¹/₄ **T.** 5/7 **P.** 1¹/₅
W. 2 **I.** 5/6 **X.** 1³/₇ **B.** 1¹/₂ **Y.** 2/3
T. 1²/₅ **E.** 4/9 **N.** 1²/₁₁ **K.** 1/2 **O.** 1¹/₄
TWENTY-SIX MILES LONG!

Page 33

1. 3/4 + 2/4 = 5/4 = 1¹/₄
2. 5/8 + 6/8 = 11/8 = 1³/₈
3. 2/3 + 3/3 = 5/3 = 1²/₃
4. 4/6 + 4/6 = 8/6 = 1²/₆ = 1¹/₃
5. 4/5 + 3/5 = 7/5 = 1²/₅
6. 5/6 + 5/6 = 10/6 = 1⁴/₆ = 1²/₃
7. 6/7 + 4/7 = 10/7 = 1³/₇
8. 7/12 + 9/12 = 16/12 = 1⁴/₁₂ = 1¹/₃
9. 7/8 + 3/8 = 10/8 = 1²/₈ = 1¹/₄
10. 8/9 + 5/9 = 13/9 = 1⁴/₉

Page 34

1. 4/10 – 1/10 = 3/10
2. 13/25 – 8/25 = 5/25 = 1/5
3. 6/8 – 4/8 = 2/8 = 1/4
4. 7/11 – 3/11 = 4/11
5. 6/7 – 4/7 = 2/7
6. 6/9 – 3/9 = 3/9 = 1/3
7. 3/5 – 2/5 = 1/5

Page 35

1. 4/9, 4/10 = 2/5, 3/12 = 1/4, 2/9, 0
2. 2/8 = 1/4, 6/14 = 3/7, 5/20 = 1/4, 3/9 = 1/3, 2/12 = 1/6
3. 8/20 = 2/5, 4/15, 6/16 = 3/8, 2/4 = 1/2, 2/15

Page 36

1. 5/8 **2.** 9/12 = 3/4 **3.** 7/10 **4.** 7/12
5. 28/32 = 7/8 **6.** 12/15 = 4/5

Page 37

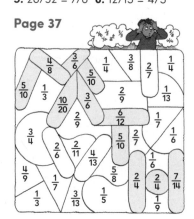

Page 38

1. 2/8 + 1/8 = 3/8, 3/9 + 1/9 = 4/9
2/10 + 1/10 = 3/10, 2/16 + 1/16 = 3/16
2. 3/12 + 1/12 = 4/12 = 1/3,
4/8 + 1/8 = 5/8, 3/15 + 1/15 = 4/15,
5/10 + 1/10 = 6/10 = 3/5
3. 2/6 + 1/6 = 3/6 = 1/2,
4/16 + 1/16 = 5/16, 4/12 + 1/12 = 5/12,
6/12 + 1/12 = 7/12
Extra Activity: 4/6 + 1/6 = 5/6 of the class

Page 39

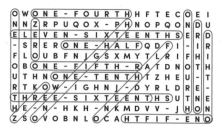

Page 40

2/6 + 1/2 = 5/6, 2/6 + 1/3 = 4/6 = 2/3;
4/12 + 1/2 = 10/12 = 5/6, 4/12 + 1/3 = 8/12 = 2/3; 4/18 + 1/2 = 13/18,
4/18 + 1/3 = 5/9
Correct path is 13/18 and 5/9.
2/12 + 1/4 = 5/12, 2/12 + 1/6 = 4/12 = 1/3; 4/36 + 1/4 = 13/36, 4/36 + 1/6 = 5/18, 4/24 + 1/4 = 10/24 = 5/12,
4/24 + 1/6 = 8/24 = 1/3
Correct path is 13/36 and 5/18.

Page 41

Y. 4/6 = 2/3 **O.** 5/12 **S.** 11/12 **U.** 5/8
G. 6/12 = 1/2 **A.** 4/9 **L.** 9/12 = 3/4
T. 3/8 **W.** 3/12 = 1/4 **F.** 5/9
M. 10/12 = 5/6 **E.** 7/10 **N.** 3/10 **R.** 7/12
!. 4/12 = 1/3 **H.** 7/8 **D.** 4/15 **I.** 4/10 = 2/5
YOU ALWAYS FINISH ON GOOD TERMS!

Page 42

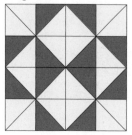

Page 43

Check students' puzzles.
Across: 3. three-fifths **5.** one-half
7. one-twelfth **8.** one-third
12. four-ninths **14.** seven-twelfths
15. one-sixth
Down: 1. one-fourth **2.** one-fourth
3. three-tenths **4.** five-twelfths
6. zero **8.** one-fifths **9.** one-tenth
10. one-fifth **11.** one-sixth **12.** zero

Page 44

1. 3/12 = 1/4 **2.** 3/16 **3.** 4/8 = 1/2
4. 11/16 **5.** 1/4 **6.** 0 **7.** 3/6 = 1/2
8. 2/6 = 1/3 **9.** 2/10 = 1/5
10. 2/16 = 1/8 **11.** 0 **12.** 2/6 = 1/3
13. 4/16 = 1/4 **14.** 1/10 **15.** 2/10 = 1/5

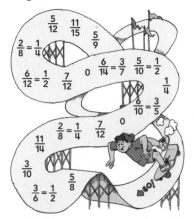

Page 45

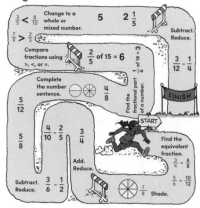

Page 46